Walking In
Divine
Destiny

FULFILLING GOD'S PURPOSE IN YOUR LIFE

STEVE WHITNEY

Copyright © 2025 Steve Whitney. All rights reserved.

Published and designed by Ministry Event Marketing.

Printed in the United States of America

ISBN: 979-8-9935218-0-0   Paperback

Disclaimer: This publication is designed to provide accurate and authoritative information regarding the subject matter covered. All materials are the intellectual property of Steve Whitney.

No part of this book may be reproduced, stored in a retrieval system, or transmitted in any form or by any means, electronic, mechanical, photocopying, recording, or otherwise, without the express written permission of the author or publisher, except by a reviewer who may quote brief passages in a review.

Unauthorized distribution, sale, or resale of any such property will result in legal action to compensate the trust for the unauthorized use of its private property.

TABLE OF CONTENTS

CHAPTER ONE:.. 1
Your Faith Will Connect You With Your Destiny

CHAPTER TWO:... 13
God Will Turn Your History Into A Story

CHAPTER THREE:.. 23
His Presence Will Change Your Destiny

CHAPTER FOUR... 33
Your Dream Will Live Again

CHAPTER FIVE... 43
Your Assignment Comes With a Fight

CHAPTER SEVEN... 49
It's Your Season to Stretch

CHAPTER EIGHT.. 57
The Cave Is Not Your Assignment

WORDS OF ENCOURAGEMENT................................. 67
You Are God's Masterpiece

CHAPTER ONE:
YOUR FAITH WILL CONNECT YOU WITH YOUR DESTINY

My Story:

There will be seasons in your life when it feels like your **faith is on trial**. To be unshakable, faith must be anchored in the **confidence that God's ultimate purpose will come to pass**.

We must trust His plan when we can't see His hand. Trust Him when we can't trace Him. Hold on to faith even when there is no relief in sight.

For seven long months, my wife and I lived in hotels—not because we were on vacation, but because we had **nowhere else to stay**. All of our personal belongings were packed in the trunk of our car. To make matters worse, our car broke down in Georgia, over 400 miles from home. We had to rent a car just to make it back to Tampa, Florida.

Every dollar we earned was going toward rental cars and extended-stay hotels. It was a heavy season. Yet through it all, I kept believing and trusting God.

We tried multiple dealerships to buy a car, but every time, we were denied. And when you're at your lowest, the enemy has a way of **whispering lies**: *"You'll never get out of this."* We bounced from hotel to hotel, trying to stretch our budget. During one of those moves, I reached my breaking point. I collapsed on the bed, sobbing like a child, crying out to the Lord, *"I can't take this anymore."*

But when you cry out to the Lord, **He answers**.

> *"In my distress I cried unto the Lord, and He heard me."* — Psalm 120:1

A Divine Connection

A few weeks later, a rental car agent who had become a friend noticed how much I was paying in rental fees. He referred me to someone he knew at a dealership. When I called, I found out that the man had left the company—but he connected me to someone else who was still there.

I called the dealership, left my name and number, and waited. A few days passed without a response, so I called again. "Can I speak to Bob?" I asked (a name I'll use to protect his identity). When Bob got on the line, I explained my situation.

"Yes," he said, "my friend told me about you. I believe I can help you. Give me a few days, and I should have an approval for you."

Two days later, he called me back **with the approval**.

Favor on Every Side

Even before this breakthrough with the car, God had already started working behind the scenes. We had previously been denied for an apartment, but God gave my wife the **favor** to go to the county court, obtain the necessary paperwork, and get approved to move in.

God didn't just open one door. He opened **multiple doors at once**. He gave us favor with the **car dealership**. He gave us favor with the **apartment manager**. And we're believing Him to do it again with our **first home**.

> God will always connect you — or use someone to connect you — to your destiny.

In our case, God used a **rental agent friend** to connect us to someone who knew Bob, the man who helped us secure the car. That's how favor works. It flows through unexpected vessels.

Faith Is the Ticket

Faith is your **ticket to destiny**. In every situation, keep praising God, keep worshiping, and keep praying.

I praise Him for what He's about to do.
I praise Him for what He's doing now.
I praise Him for what He's already done.

About two years ago, I received a letter in the mail. It read:

> *"This letter is to inform Steve Whitney that your outstanding loan of $96,000 has been paid in full."*

I didn't pay it. No one I knew paid it. **Nobody but God**.

And the incredible part? The loan had been paid off six months earlier. All that time, while

I was praising God, He had already done the work. That's the kind of God we serve. While you are praising Him, **He is working behind the scenes for you**.

The Final Say

Even when your faith feels like it's on trial, **never forget who the Judge is**.

The Judge—your Father in heaven—has the final say.

When I was living out of hotels and driving rental cars, I **never stopped praising and worshiping God**. I had seen Him do the impossible before. If God could **cancel a $96,000 debt**, I knew He could bring my wife and me out of any situation.

And He did.

If God did it for us, He can—and will—do it for you, too.

Where you've been denied, **go back and try again**.

Never give up.

> *"For with God nothing shall be impossible."* — Luke 1:37

These are some scriptures that keep me grounded in my faith.

> *Without faith it's impossible to please Him: for he that cometh to God must believe that he is, and he is a rewarder to them that diligently seek Him. Hebrews 11:6*

> *Now unto Him that is able to do exceedingly abundantly above all that we can ask or think, according to the power that worketh in us. Ephesians 3:20*

> *Now faith is the substance of things hoped for, the evidence of things not seen. Hebrews 11:1*

> *Jesus said unto him, If thou canst believe, all things are possible to him that believeth. The father of the child cried out with tears. Lord, I believe, but help my unbelief. His disciples ask*

Him privately, "Why could not we cast him out? Jesus said unto them, This kind can only come forth by prayer and fasting. Mark 9:23

Finally, my brethren, be strong in the Lord and in the power of his might. Put on the whole armor of God, that ye might be able to stand against the wiles of the evil. For we wrestle not against flesh and blood, but against principalities, against powers of darkness of this world, against spiritual weakness in high places. Wherefore take unto you the whole armor of God. You may be able to withstand in the evil day, and having done all to stand. Stand therefore, having your loins girt with truth and on the breastplate of righteousness, and your feet shod with the preparation of the gospel of peace, above all, taking the shield of faith.

Therefore, you will be able to quench all the fiery darts of the wicked and take the helmet of salvation and the sword of the Spirit, which is the word of God. Ephesians 6:16.

Faith is part of the armor, and you must have on your armor to fight. You must have on your armor to connect to your destiny.

CHAPTER TWO:
GOD WILL TURN YOUR HISTORY INTO A STORY

Before his encounter with Christ, Paul's mission was to persecute believers of the early Church. His history was marked by opposition, hostility, and violence toward followers of Jesus. Yet it was this same man whom God would transform into one of the greatest apostles in history.

The Bible records in **Acts 7: 58–60**:

"Then they cried with a loud voice, stopped their ears, and ran upon him with

one accord, and cast him out of the city, and stoned him. And the witnesses laid down their clothes at a young man's feet, whose name was Saul. And they stoned Stephen, calling upon God and saying, 'Lord Jesus, receive my spirit.' And he kneeled down, and cried with a loud voice, 'Lord, lay not this sin to their charge.' And when he had said this, he fell asleep."

This moment is the first mention of Saul—later called Paul—whose life would have a greater impact on Christianity than any other individual apart from Christ Himself. The death of Stephen was a pivotal event that would echo through Paul's future. God was already setting the stage to **turn history into a testimony**.

A Divine Interruption

Paul recounts his conversion in **Acts 26:12–16**:

> *"On one of these journeys, I was going to Damascus with the authority and commission of the chief priests. At midday, O king, I saw a light from heaven, brighter than the sun, blazing around me and my companions. We all fell to the ground, and I heard a voice saying to me in Aramaic, 'Saul, Saul, why are you persecuting Me? It is hard for you to kick against the goads.' Then I asked, 'Who are You, Lord?' 'I am Jesus, whom you are persecuting,' the Lord replied. 'Now get up and stand on your feet. I have appeared to you to appoint you as a servant and as a witness of what you have*

seen and will see of Me.'"

On the road to Damascus, Saul's **path of destruction collided with God's plan of redemption**. In a single encounter, everything changed. Saul, the persecutor, became Paul, the apostle. His **history became his story**, and his story became a message that would lead multitudes to Christ.

When God Changes Your Name

When God turns your history into a story, He often gives you a **new identity**. Throughout Scripture, name changes mark **new assignments and destinies**:

- **Abram** became **Abraham** — "Father of many nations."
- **Sarai** became **Sarah** — "Princess."

- **Jacob** became **Israel** — "God prevails."

In each case, God wasn't just changing a name; He was **announcing a new season**. When Jacob wrestled with the angel, his name was changed to Israel, signifying not just a victory but a new purpose and position before God.

Likewise, Saul became Paul—a name associated not with persecution, but with grace, apostleship, and purpose.

Your Damascus Road

You may be on your own journey to Damascus. Maybe your path has been marked by pain, mistakes, or detours. But the same God who met Saul on the road is able to **interrupt your travels and turn you in the right direction**.

> *"But now thus says the Lord who created you, O Jacob, and He who formed you, O Israel: 'Fear not, for I have redeemed you; I have called you by your name; you are Mine. When you pass through the waters, I will be with you; and through the rivers, they shall not overflow you. When you walk through the fire, you shall not be burned, nor shall the flame scorch you.'"*
> — Isaiah 43:1-2

No matter what you're facing, **God can turn it around**. He specializes in rewriting stories. What looks like a dead end can become the birthplace of your testimony.

Keys to Reaching Your Destiny

Three major keys will carry you into your God-ordained destiny:

1. **Obedience** — Say yes to God even when the path is unclear.
2. **Faith** — Believe that His Word will accomplish what He promised.
3. **Action** — Take steps toward what God has called you to do.

I've learned that walking in divine purpose requires all three. It's not enough to simply believe; you must **move**. Your obedience positions you. Your faith sustains you. Your actions unlock doors.

There will be seasons when your **faith feels like it's on trial**, but even then—trust Him.

Believe what He says. Praise Him through the pressure. God is faithful to walk you through every situation.

God Is Writing Your Story

Whatever you are facing today—fear, pressure, doubt, or pain—God is saying:

> *"Don't be afraid. Stay faithful. I've got you."*

Every storm you endure has the power to shape your character and strengthen your faith. You are not walking alone. God is with you. He is cheering you on, equipping you with strength, and preparing you for what's ahead.

Your **past does not define you**; it prepares you.

Your **history is not the end**; it's the raw material God uses to build your testimony.

Always remember: **God is fulfilling His purpose in your problem.**

Just as He did for Paul, God will take what was meant for your destruction and turn it into the foundation of your destiny. **Your history will become His story.**

CHAPTER THREE:

His Presence Will Change Your Destiny

In the Gospel of John, chapter four, Jesus was on His way to Galilee. On this journey, **He had to pass through Samaria**, a place that held a divine appointment. It was there that He met **the woman at the well**, an encounter that would change not only her life but the destiny of an entire city.

> *"The hour comes when you shall neither in this mountain nor yet at Jerusalem worship the Father. You worship what you do not know; we know what we worship,*

for salvation is of the Jews. But the hour comes, and now is, when the true worshippers shall worship the Father in spirit and in truth. For the Father seeks such to worship Him." (John 4:21-23)

Jesus revealed to her that **true worship is not about a location—it is about the posture of the heart**. The Holy Spirit had led Him to Samaria because there were hungry hearts waiting to encounter the Messiah. When the woman later ran into the city crying, *"Come see a man,"* it became evident that they had been searching for the One who could satisfy their thirst.

The Power of Worship and His Presence

Worship is more than singing a song; it is **a sacred act of reverence, respect, and adoration** for the living God. Jesus was teaching the woman at the well that it isn't **where** we worship, but **who** we worship that matters most.

Throughout Scripture, we see how **God's presence transforms everything it touches**:

- In *1 Kings 19*, the Lord said to Elijah, *"Go forth and stand on the mountain in the presence of the Lord, for the Lord is about to pass by."*
- *Psalm 67* describes the shining of God's face as the manifestation of His presence.
- *Joshua 1:5* reminds us that the downcast find strength and encouragement when they seek Him.

- In *2 Samuel 21*, David sought the Lord's presence during a famine, and God heard him.

The presence of God is not passive. **It moves, heals, restores, and realigns destinies.** When you come in contact with His presence, you will never be the same.

A Destiny Shift at the Well

When Jesus approached the well, He asked the Samaritan woman, *"Give Me something to drink."* This request shocked her. Jews did not speak to Samaritans, much less ask them for a favor. *"How is it that you, being a Jew, ask a drink of me, a woman of Samaria?"* she asked.

Jesus responded, *"If you knew the gift of God, and who it is that says to you, 'Give Me to drink,' you would have asked Him, and He would have given you living water."*

He explained that those who drink natural water will thirst again, but those who drink the water He gives will never thirst; it will become a well springing up into everlasting life. The woman, intrigued and hungry, said, *"Sir, give me this water."*

Jesus then revealed her truth: she had five husbands, and the man she was with was not her husband. Stunned, she replied, *"I perceive that you are a prophet."* She acknowledged the coming of the Messiah, and Jesus declared, *"I who speak to you am He."*

The woman left her waterpot behind and ran into the city, crying out, *"Come see a man who told me everything I ever did. Is not this the Christ?"*

One encounter with His presence changed her life and, through her testimony, transformed a city.

Whatever you need is found in His presence. If you need peace, it's in His presence. If you need healing, it's in His presence. If you need deliverance, it's in His presence. If you need a financial breakthrough, it's in His presence. If you need salvation, just like the woman at the well, it's in His presence.

God's Presence Is Everywhere

God is Spirit. He is not confined to buildings, temples, or mountains. His presence is

everywhere at all times. That is why **the place** is not what matters—**the posture** does. True worship begins in spirit and truth.

> *"Likewise, the Spirit also helps our infirmities; for we know not what we should pray for as we ought, but the Spirit itself maketh intercession for us with groanings which cannot be uttered."* (Romans 8:26)

When you encounter Jesus, your destiny cannot remain the same.

The Woman with the Issue of Blood

In *Luke 8*, Jesus was on His way to Jairus's house to heal his dying daughter when a woman who had suffered from an issue of blood for twelve years pressed through the crowd. She had spent everything she had, and by law, she wasn't even allowed to be in public. But she **took a risk**.

> *"She said to herself, If I can just touch the hem of His garment, I will be made whole."*

She touched Him, and **instantly** she was healed. Jesus turned and asked, *"Who touched Me?"* Peter tried to explain that the crowd was pressing in, but Jesus said, *"I felt power go out of Me."* Trembling, the woman came forward and testified. Jesus said, *"Daughter, your faith has healed you. Go in peace."*

One touch in His presence changed everything.

Miracle at the Lake

In *Luke 5*, the disciples were exhausted after fishing all night and catching nothing. Then Jesus showed up and said, *"Cast your nets on the other side."* Simon replied, *"Master, we've toiled all night and caught nothing. But at Your word, I will let down the nets."*

When they obeyed, their nets overflowed with so many fish that they began to break. When Jesus shows up, lack is replaced by abundance. **Atmospheres shift. Destinies change.**

Your Destiny Changes in His Presence

Just like the Samaritan woman at the well, the woman with the issue of blood, and the disciples by the lake, **everything changes when you encounter His presence**.

- Burdens are lifted.
- Chains are broken.
- Lives are transformed.
- Dreams are resurrected.

God's presence is not a distant concept. It is a **living reality** that invades spaces, touches hearts, and redirects destinies. One moment with Jesus can accomplish what years of striving cannot.

> *"In Your presence is fullness of joy; at Your right hand are pleasures forevermore."* (Psalm 16:11)

CHAPTER FOUR

Your Dream Will Live Again

When a dream dies, it can feel like the very breath has left your purpose. But God is the giver of life, and He specializes in resurrection. When your dream dies, He will either give you the **power to speak life into it** or send a **destiny helper** to help bring it back to life.

There are several **keys** that open spiritual doors. One of the most powerful of these is **honor**, a principle beautifully illustrated in the story of the **Shunammite woman** in 2 Kings 4.

> *"And she said to her husband, Behold now, I perceive that this is a holy man of*

God, which passeth by us continually. Let us make a little chamber, I pray thee, on the wall; and let us set for him there a bed, and a table, and a stool, and a candlestick: and it shall be, when he cometh to us, that he shall turn in thither." (2 Kings 4:9-10)

This woman discerned that the man passing by her home was a holy man of God. She honored him by building a room for him, creating a sacred space for divine encounters. Her act of honor positioned her for a miracle she hadn't even asked for.

When Elisha asked what could be done for her, she replied, "I dwell among my own people." But Gehazi, Elisha's servant, observed that she had no children and her husband was old.

Elisha called for her, and she came and stood in the doorway.

The **doorway** is not just a physical space. It represents a **portal**, a threshold between where you are and where God is taking you. When you **stand in the place God has called you to**, that threshold becomes the bridge to your destiny.

Elisha prophesied, "About this season, according to the time of life, you shall embrace a son." At first, she could hardly believe it. "No, my lord," she said. "Do not lie to your handmaid." Yet at the appointed time, she conceived and gave birth to a son, just as the prophet had spoken.

When the Promise Seems to Die

Years later, her miracle faced its greatest test. While in the field with his father, the boy suddenly cried out, "My head! My head!" He was carried home to his mother and sat on her lap until noon. Then, he died.

Most people would have collapsed in despair. But this woman did something extraordinary. She **carried the child upstairs**, laid him on the prophet's bed, **shut the door**, and left him there. She didn't bury him. She didn't wail or panic. She held on to the promise. She sent word to her husband: "Send me one of the servants and a donkey so I can go quickly to the man of God and return."

When she approached Mount Carmel, Elisha saw her in the distance and sent his servant to ask, "Is everything all right with you, your husband, and your child?" Her reply was both simple and profound: **"All is well."**

How could she say that when her son lay lifeless on a bed? Because she **honored God**, and she **believed** that the promise was not over.

When Elisha arrived, he went into the room alone, shut the door, and prayed. Then he lay on the child, mouth to mouth, eyes to eyes, hands to hands. As he stretched out on him, the child's body grew warm. Elisha walked back and forth, then stretched out on the child again. The boy sneezed seven times and opened his eyes.

The promise lived again.

Her dream—her miracle—came back to life because she honored the man of God and held fast to faith.

Four More Keys to Unlock Spiritual Doors

1. The Key of Knowledge

> *"For the Lord gives wisdom; from His mouth come knowledge and understanding."* — Proverbs 2:6

Knowledge is a spiritual key. What you know determines how far you can go. God imparts wisdom that unlocks doors no man can shut.

2. The Key of Faith

> *"Now faith is confidence in what we hope for and assurance about what we do not see."* — Hebrews 11:1
>
> *"And whatever you ask in prayer, you*

> *will receive, if you have faith."* — Matthew 21:22
>
> *"For nothing will be impossible with God."* — Luke 1:37
>
> *"So faith comes from hearing, and hearing through the word of Christ."* — Romans 10:17

Faith is the bridge between the unseen and the seen. It fuels miracles, sustains hope, and turns promises into reality.

3. The Key of Favor

> *"And Joseph found favor in his sight, and he served him; and he made him overseer over his house, and all that he had he put into his hand."* — Genesis 39:4

Favor is God's way of accelerating your journey. You unlock favor by keeping God first—by living a life of obedience, humility, and honor. Favor is when someone decides to participate in your success.

> *"And Jesus grew in wisdom and stature, and in favor with God and man."* — Luke 2:52

Favor dries tears, silences fear, and moves mountains. It's when someone believes in you, sees a need, and chooses to meet it.

Daniel had favor with God.

The three Hebrew boys had favor with God.

Paul and Silas had favor with God.

And **you** can too.

Hold On to Your Dream

Never give up on your dream. Your dream is your **ticket to destiny**. Along the way, you will encounter dream killers—people or circumstances designed to derail your vision. But you must stand firm. Guard your vision. Protect your promise.

To conquer your dream, you must carry the **heart of a warrior**:

A warrior doesn't quit.

A warrior stands tall in the storm.

A warrior is strong, confident, secure, courageous, victorious, and grateful.

God is not finished with your story.
What looks dead can live again.
Your dream will live again.

CHAPTER FIVE

Your Assignment Comes With a Fight

Be who God created you to be.

In **1 Samuel 17**, the Bible tells the story of a young shepherd named **David**, who faced the giant **Goliath** when no one else would. Before stepping into the fight, King Saul tried to give David his own armor—a helmet of brass, a coat of mail, and his weapons.

But David refused.

> *"I cannot go with these," he said to Saul. "I have not proved them."*

David took off the armor because he

understood something powerful: **you cannot fight your battle wearing someone else's identity**. Your assignment comes with its own weapons, not borrowed ones.

The Power of Preparedness

The Bible says David went down to the brook, chose five smooth stones, and placed them in his shepherd's bag. With only his sling in his hand, David stepped onto the battlefield. He didn't rely on Saul's armor—he relied on his **faith**.

David remembered the lion and the bear that had once come to attack his father's flock. He told Saul,

> *"The Lord who delivered me from the paw of the lion and the paw of the bear will*

deliver me from the hand of this Philistine." — 1 Samuel 17:37

His confidence wasn't in the stone. His confidence was in **God**.

When the moment came, David reached into his bag, took out a stone, slung it, and struck Goliath in the forehead. The stone sank deep, and the giant fell face down to the ground.

"So David prevailed over the Philistine with a sling and a stone." — 1 Samuel 17:50

David had no sword in his hand, yet God gave him the victory. **God is not limited by the weapon. He is empowered by your faith.**

Decree, Declare, and Defeat

To walk in your assignment, you must **decree and declare** that what God has spoken over your life will come to pass.

- Be who God created you to be.
- Put on your **own armor**.
- Remember the victories God has already given you.
- Pray for strength.
- Stand ready for the moment.

David didn't just show up to the battlefield—he was **prepared for it**. He had practiced in private what God would use in public. The lion and the bear were preparation for the giant.

Faith That Fights

David looked back at past victories, focused on the present giant, and moved forward in faith. He didn't just pick up a stone—he picked up **evidence of his preparation**.

Just as Saul and the men of Israel were facing a situation, **David was the answer** God sent. Likewise, your assignment is often connected to **solving someone else's problem**. When your giant appears, it's not a sign of defeat—it's a sign that **your assignment has arrived**.

- Be prepared.
- Be an answer.
- Be bold.

David didn't wait for someone else to step up. He stepped forward and **slew his giant**.

The Giant Is the Gateway

Find something bigger than yourself to conquer. There is a **king in you** waiting to be revealed on the other side of your giant.

- **Kill your giant and you'll discover your domain.**
- **Kill your giant, and doors will open.**
- **Kill your giant, and destiny will unfold.**

Don't run from your giant. Go get your giant. **Don't keep your giant waiting.** God has equipped you with everything you need to fulfill your assignment. Your sling may look small, but in the hands of faith, it's a weapon of victory.

CHAPTER SEVEN

It's Your Season to Stretch

Stretching will take you to your **destiny**. When you stretch, you **expand your capacity**, your ability to step into something you've never done before. Stretching is not always comfortable, but it is always purposeful. It is in the stretch that faith grows, obedience is tested, and miracles are birthed.

Stretching Beyond Limitations

"And it came to pass also on another Sabbath, that he entered into the synagogue and taught: and there was a man whose right hand was withered. And

the scribes and Pharisees watched him, whether he would heal on the sabbath day; that they might find an accusation against him. But he knew their thoughts, and said to the man which had the withered hand, Rise up, and stand forth in the midst. And he arose and stood forth... And looking round about upon them all, he said unto the man, Stretch forth thy hand. And he did so: and his hand was restored whole as the other." — Luke 6: 6-8, 10

The man with the withered hand represents what it means to be **stuck in limitation**. His right hand was crippled—a part of him had lost its function. Yet, when Jesus called him forward, he **responded with faith and obedience**.

- He rose up.
- He came forth.
- He stretched out.

And because he stretched, his hand was **restored**.

> It takes **faith**, **action**, and **obedience** to stretch.

"Withered" means to decay, disintegrate, or decline. Maybe your situation feels withered right now—your dream, your finances, your joy, or your strength. But in the **presence of God**, with faith and obedience, everything can change.

The Bible specifically notes that it was his **right hand**, a symbol of **authority and power**. The enemy loves to attack us at the place of our strength, the place of our gifting. But when Jesus steps in, what was withered is **revived**, and what was broken is **restored**.

In His presence:

- Emotions are healed.
- Fear, depression, and suicidal chains are broken.
- Strongholds are destroyed.

Chains keep you from stretching, but once you stretch, **your mind can never go back to its original size**.

Moses Had to Stretch

Stretching isn't new. Moses had to stretch too.

> "And Moses stretched out his hand over the sea; and the Lord caused the sea to go

back by a strong east wind all that night, and made the sea dry land, and the waters were divided." — Exodus 14:21

With faith, obedience, and action, Moses **stretched out his hand** and God split the Red Sea. The children of Israel walked on dry ground, surrounded by walls of water on their left and right. When Moses stretched again, the sea closed, swallowing their enemies.

God didn't move until Moses stretched. **The miracle was in the stretch.**

Stretching Through Prayer

Stretching requires a **life of prayer**. Prayer builds faith. Prayer strengthens obedience. Prayer ignites action.

In Daniel 3, the **three Hebrew boys** stretched their faith when they refused to bow to the king's idol. They were thrown into the fiery furnace—but when they stretched their faith, the **Fourth Man showed up**.

In Daniel 6, Daniel stretched his faith in the lions' den. He prayed, and **God shut the mouths of lions**.

> *"No weapon formed against you shall prosper."* — Isaiah 54:17

My prayer for you is that **God will dispatch His angels** to shut the mouths of the lions coming against you. He will be the **Fourth Man in your fire**. You will not be consumed. Your stretch will lead to victory.

It's Time to Stretch

This is your season to **stretch your faith**, **stretch your mind**, and **stretch your obedience**.

- Stretch beyond fear.
- Stretch beyond doubt.
- Stretch beyond limitation.

When you stretch, you partner with God's purpose. When you stretch, He steps in with power. The stretch is uncomfortable, but it is also **transformational**. Stretching will take you to your **next dimension of destiny**.

.

CHAPTER EIGHT

THE CAVE IS NOT YOUR ASSIGNMENT

A cave is a hollow place beneath the ground dark, isolated, and quiet. It's a place where a person can hide away from the world. But spiritually, **the cave can represent a place of retreat, depression, fear, or discouragement**.

There are moments in life when pain, anger, fear, and weariness push us into a spiritual cave. But while the cave may be where you **pause**, it is **not where you belong**. The cave is not your assignment.

Elijah's Cave

In **1 Kings 18**, the prophet Elijah stood in power and boldness. He called down fire from heaven to prove that Yahweh is the only true God.

> *"Then the fire of the Lord fell, and consumed the burnt sacrifice, and the wood, and the stones, and the dust, and licked up the water that was in the trench. And when all the people saw it, they fell on their faces: and they said, The Lord, he is the God; the Lord, he is the God."* — 1 Kings 18:38-39

Elijah also declared, *"There is the sound of abundance of rain."* (1 Kings 18:41) He prayed, and the heavens responded. Rain fell. The hand of the Lord came upon Elijah, and he outran Ahab's chariot all the way to Jezreel.

This was a **mountain-top moment,** a moment of undeniable victory. Yet immediately after such a powerful demonstration, **the enemy attacked**.

Fear That Sends You Running

When Jezebel heard of Elijah's victory, she sent a threat:

> *"So let the gods do to me, and more also, if I make not thy life as the life of one of them by tomorrow about this time."* — 1 Kings 19:2

Fear entered Elijah's heart. He fled for his life, leaving his servant behind, and journeyed into the wilderness. The mighty prophet, who had just called down fire, now found himself running in fear.

He sat under a juniper tree, exhausted, and cried out to God:

> *"It is enough; now, O Lord, take away my life."* — 1 Kings 19:4

But God didn't rebuke him. He **sent an angel** with food and water. Twice, the angel touched him and said, *"Arise and eat, because the journey is too great for thee."* (1 Kings 19:7)

Strengthened, Elijah traveled to **a cave** and lodged there. And then came the voice of the Lord: *"What are you doing here, Elijah?"* 1 Kings 19:9

When God asks a question, He already knows the answer. He asked Adam, *"Where are you?"*

He asked Moses, *"What is that in your hand?"* And here, He asks Elijah, *"What are you doing here?"*

God didn't lead Elijah to the cave; **Elijah led himself there**.

The Still Small Voice

Elijah poured out his complaint, saying he was the only prophet left. Then God revealed Himself—not in the wind, not in the earthquake, not in the fire—but in a **still small voice**. (1 Kings 19:11-12)

God asked Elijah the same question again:

"What are you doing here, Elijah?"

And then came the command:

> *"Go, return on thy way to the wilderness of Damascus: and when thou comest, anoint Hazael to be king over Syria."*
>
> — 1 Kings 19:15

God had **an assignment waiting outside the cave**. He reminded Elijah of his mission, not his fear. Elijah was called to anoint Hazael as king and to find Elisha, the one who would carry the mantle forward.

Your Cave Is Not Your Destiny

Maybe today, like Elijah, you find yourself in a **cave of fear, depression, or exhaustion**. Perhaps the battle has been long, the warfare intense, and the weight overwhelming.

But the Lord is still asking: *"What are you doing here?"*

Your cave is not your assignment. Your calling is not in the dark. The Lord is still speaking **in the still small voice**, giving direction for your next move.

Elijah's next step was to **return**. To get out of the cave. To walk back into destiny.

Getting Out of the Cave

How do you get out of the cave? You do what the early church did:

- **Pray.** When Paul and Silas prayed, prison doors opened.
- **Worship.** When the church prayed for Peter, chains fell, and the Lord set him

free.

- **Stand in faith.** When the three Hebrew boys prayed, the Fourth Man showed up.
- **Trust.** When Daniel prayed, God shut the mouths of lions.
- **Believe.** When I cried out in my own dark season, God showed up and delivered me.

Whatever cave you're in, God is able to pull you out.

Fear seeks to **isolate**, but faith draws you **into your assignment**. The cave is not your destiny. The cave is not your purpose. The cave is not where the story ends.

Arise and Return

Just like Elijah, your journey isn't over. There is **an assignment waiting** on the other side of your cave. There are people to impact, prayers to pray, battles to win, and mantles to release.

> God is saying: "Arise. Return. Step back into your calling."

This is your moment to get up, dust off discouragement, and step out of the hollow place. You were not created to live in hiding. **You were created to walk in power.**

The cave is not your assignment. Destiny is calling your name.

WORDS OF ENCOURAGEMENT

You Are God's Masterpiece

"So God created human beings in His own image. In the image of God He created them; male and female He created them." — **Genesis 1:27**

"The Lord has declared today that you are His people, His own special treasure, just as He promised, and that you must obey all His commands." — **Deuteronomy 26:18**

"Yet You made them only a little lower than God and crowned them with glory and honor." — **Psalm 8:5**

"And what do you benefit if you gain the

whole world but lose your own soul? Is anything worth more than your soul?" — **Matthew 16:26**

"For we are God's masterpiece. He has created us anew in Christ Jesus, so we can do the good things He planned for us long ago." — **Ephesians 2:10**

God made you in His image. He values you highly—so much so that He sent His Son to die for your sins. You are His treasure. His masterpiece. His beloved.

> *"You made all the delicate, inner parts of my body and knit me together in my mother's womb."* — **Psalm 139:13**
>
> *"I knew you before I formed you in your mother's womb. Before you were born, I set you apart and appointed you as my

prophet to the nations." — **Jeremiah 1:5**

God crafted you with skill and loving care. Every detail of your existence carries His intentional design. **You are invaluable.**

Strength in the Storm

"Blessed is the one who perseveres under trial because, having stood the test, that person will receive the crown of life that the Lord has promised to those who love Him." — **James 1:12**

Life isn't always easy. Trials will come. Some weeks will feel heavier than others. But **James 1:12** reminds us that blessing is on the other side of perseverance.

God sees the tears you cry in silence. He

knows the weight you carry. But if you hold on, keep the faith, and don't let go—you'll receive a crown of life, not just for surviving the storm, but for **trusting Him through it**.

Don't let the pressure make you forget who you are. You've already survived things you thought would break you. The same God who brought you through then is carrying you now.

Let this season be a **reset**, a reminder that you're stronger than the trial and more blessed than the burden. You're not stuck; you're being strengthened.

God Is Standing Beside You

"But the Lord stood at my side and gave me strength." — **2 Timothy 4:17**

Even the strongest among us experience

moments of loneliness. The apostle Paul knew this well. Everyone deserted him, yet the Lord stood by his side and gave him the strength to keep going.

Let this be your reminder: Even when it feels like no one understands or supports you, **God stands beside you**.

- He is your defender when you are wronged.
- He is your strength when you are weary.
- He is your peace in the middle of confusion.

You are never alone when the Almighty is in your corner.

Delivered From Them All

"Many are the afflictions of the righteous: but the Lord delivers him out of them all."
— **Psalm 34:19**

Life brings trials, some expected, others not. But God promises **deliverance from them all**.

Hard times don't mean God has abandoned you. They are often the moments where He is preparing your breakthrough. **Hold firm**, God's rescue is on the way.

You are closer to your breakthrough than you think. Every challenge is shaping your strength, refining your faith, and revealing your resilience.

Say to yourself: **"God is not done with me yet. This obstacle is just a setup for**

something greater."

Prayers to Strengthen Your Journey

A Prayer for Endurance

Lord, thank You for being my strength when I'm weak and my hope when I feel overwhelmed. I pray for endurance through every trial and a heart that trusts You even when the way isn't clear. As I step into a new day, help me to rest, reflect, and reconnect with Your purpose for my life. Remind me that my trials are temporary, but Your promises are eternal. Crown me with peace, joy, and strength. In Jesus' name, Amen.

A Prayer for Boldness and Strength

Heavenly Father, thank You for the

promise that You stand by me. In moments of loneliness, remind me I am never alone. Strengthen me as You strengthened Paul. Help me to speak boldly, act courageously, and live faithfully, knowing You are with me every step I take. Let Your presence be my peace, and Your power be my push forward. In Jesus' name, Amen.

A Prayer for Grace and Humility

Heavenly Father, thank You for another day and for the blessing of a new month. Your Word says You give more grace, and I need it. Help me to walk humbly today and always — not in weakness, but in trust of Your strength. Keep me from pride that separates me from Your favor. Teach me to rely on You in every decision and every moment. Let my words, actions, and attitude reflect the heart of someone shaped by Your grace. Surround me with peace, lead me in wisdom, and let this day, this month, and this year be filled with moments that glorify You. In Jesus' name, Amen.

A Prayer for Trusting God's Timing

Heavenly Father, thank You for the promise in Habakkuk 2. Help me trust in Your perfect timing, even when I can't see what You are doing. Strengthen my faith while I wait. Let me not grow weary but keep my eyes on You. I surrender my impatience, my doubts, and my fears. Today I choose to walk in peace, knowing that what You have spoken over my life will not fail. In Jesus' name, Amen.

The Prayer of Salvation

"Dear God, I come to You today as a sinner, acknowledging my need for forgiveness. I believe that Jesus Christ died on the cross for my sins and that He rose again. I confess that Jesus is Lord, and I believe in my heart that God raised Him from the dead. I now ask Jesus to come into my heart and be my Lord and Savior. Please forgive me and cleanse me of my sins. I thank You for Your grace and Your salvation. Amen."

Powerful Financial Decrees

(Unusual and Expanded Declarations)

"And Elijah said unto Ahab, Get thee up,

eat and drink; for there is a sound of abundance of rain." — **1 Kings 18:41**

I decree: **Abundance of rain comes to my life.** All financial drought has ended. Just as Elijah heard the sound of an abundance of rain, I hear the sound of breakthrough and provision echoing over my life.

- The famine of lack, delay, and insufficiency is over.
- The heavens are opened over me, and the rain of God's provision is pouring out in abundance.
- Fresh rain waters every dry place in my finances.
- Dry wells are filled. Empty accounts are replenished. Stagnant dreams are revived.

I decree that the rain of abundance falls on:

- My business and career
- My investments and properties
- Every venture my hands touch

I decree **multiplication, acceleration,** and **supernatural supply**.

The clouds heavy with blessing now empty themselves over my life.

I live under open heavens—not under brass skies of frustration or scarcity.

- The rain brings forth my harvest.
- The rain brings forth new opportunities.
- The rain brings forth the manifestation of every prophetic promise spoken over my finances.

I decree:

- Debts are canceled.
- Bills are paid.
- New streams of income are born.
- Financial miracles overflow in my life.

I am not scraping by, I am overflowing.

I am not in a survival model; I am living in an **abundant blessing mode**.

I hear the sound of rain, and I see the manifestation. Every area that was once barren is now fruitful. Every delay is turned into divine delivery. Every dryness is turned into refreshing.

This is my season of abundance. This is my season of rain.

www.ingramcontent.com/pod-product-compliance
Lightning Source LLC
Chambersburg PA
CBHW071228160426
43196CB00012B/2447